Marco Sievers

No translation is perfect

Gain and loss of linguistic and cultural features

Marco Sievers

No translation is perfect

Gain and loss of linguistic and cultural features

GRIN Verlag

Bibliografische Information der Deutschen Nationalbibliothek: Die Deutsche Bibliothek
verzeichnet diese Publikation in der Deutschen Nationalbibliografie; detaillierte bibliografische Daten sind im Internet über http://dnb.d-nb.de/ abrufbar.

1. Auflage 2006
Copyright © 2006 GRIN Verlag
http://www.grin.com/
Druck und Bindung: Books on Demand GmbH, Norderstedt Germany
ISBN 978-3-638-83144-4

Liverpool John Moores University
Faculty of Business & Law
School of Languages
Translation Studies
LNG**GE** 3031

Coursework

No Translation is perfect. Gain and Loss of Linguistic and Cultural Features are Inevitable.

Submitted by:
Marco Sievers

The basic assumption of laymen concerning translation is that every word or meaning can universally be translated from one language to another. Their idea of translation is that of a straightforward mechanical process which simply replaces source language (SL) items with target language (TL) items. Some conceptions in translation studies seem to encourage this view, and debates suggest that it is only a matter of the right scope, focus or technique to create perfect translations.

The paper at hand will refute this notion. It will prove and exemplify the facts that not everything is translatable, and that a transfer of meaning necessarily involves changes entailing loss or gain of linguistic, cultural and stylistic features (cf. Harvey 2001, 38; Pym & Turk 2001, 274). Translation cannot create an identical TL copy of the SL text, but only permits a relative equivalence to it. A maximal approximation, however, can never be achieved, due to the complexity of language, its dependence on constantly changing cultural norms, and because the human factor. Especially the aspect acceptance by the audience will show that perfection is just an abstract evaluative term, which largely depends on individual taste.

According to the Longman Dictionary of Contemporary English, perfection is the state of being perfect, which in turn can be described as the absence of mistakes and faults, or as good as possible (Summers 2003, CD-ROM entries). But what does this term imply for translation? Flawlessness could be regarded as total sameness in the sense that the translated text is an identical one-to-one copy of the source text. In this vein the notion of a literal or gloss translation assumes that an ideal translation can be achieved by a segmentation of the SL text into individual words and by transferring these word-segments one at a time (cf. Robinson 2001, 125). This might work with simple grammatical patterns, as the translation of the English sentence *Peter took the book* into the German *Peter nahm das Buch* illustrates. But already slightly more complex structures lead to ungrammatical or at least unnatural or clumsy results. The translation of *Peter has taken the book from the desk* into * *Peter hat genommen das Buch von dem Schreibtisch* shows that a syntactic modification is necessary to form the grammatical sentence *Peter hat das Buch von dem Schreibtisch genommen*. Thus, "translation is no formal procedure of substitution on the basis of simple one-to-one correspondences" (Wilss 2001, 58) which could yield an identical TL text. Due to this, sameness cannot constitute perfection in terms of translation.

As a relative norm perfection can be seen as a maximum convergence of a translation to the original. In this case the notion of equivalence of SL and TL text is the main criterion for translation. Equivalence is the relationship between a source text (ST) and a target text

1

(TT) which allows the TT to be considered a translation of the ST (cf. Kenny 2001, 77). Equivalence can exist on different levels, for instance as linguistic equivalence, referring to lexis, grammar and pragmatics, as cultural or as stylistic equivalence. Basically, a translation must be adapted to the TL and its cultural norms to use equivalent pragmatic means which ensure that the TT creates the same response in TL receptors like the ST did in SL receptors. (cf. Kenny 2001, 77 et seq.; House 2001, 197 et seq.). Perfection would assume a maximum of equivalence on all levels, but such a maximum can never be achieved due to the complexity of language, its dependence on constantly changing cultural norm, and because of the human factor in form of translators and receptors. These factors inevitably lead to modifications of the SL text including loss or gain of lexical, grammatical, cultural or stylistic features.

Language itself it very complex, but difficulties increase exponentially in translation, since it has to cope with two languages. The degree of translatability basically depends on the structural differences between SL and TL (cf. Pym & Turk 2001, 274). If equivalence should be achieved, obligatory shifts have to be made in order to allow for language constraints (cf. BAKKER, KOSTER, VAN LEUVEN-ZWART 2001, 228 et seq.).

Certain lexical items or grammatical structures may only exist in one language but not in the other. Certain words have no TL equivalent, since the concept that they contain is unknown in the TL culture. For instance, a TL culture that does not know the concept 'cheese' will have no correspondent word for it. This lack can be compensated by paraphrasing or by using calques, or just by using the SL word and describing it in a footnote. *Cheese* for example can be described as 'coagulated milk curds' (cf. Pym & Turk 2001, 275). Nevertheless, do paraphrasing and the use of calques entail a loss of SL precision and make the meaning of words more elusive. Furthermore, the usage of SL words is no true translation, even if it may lead to the creation of TL loanwords. Finally, an explanation in footnotes is a deviation from the SL text in form of surplus information. Examples of words in German that demand some kind of elucidation are *Einwohnermeldeamt* or *Personenregister*, since the British and Anglo-American culture does not know such institutions. On the other hand words like *Schadenfreude, Rucksack,* and *Kindergarten* are examples of German words which became loanwords in English due to the former uniqueness of their concepts.

Also grammatical structures may exist in the SL, but not in the TL. The gerund in English for instance has no German counterpart. Therefore a translation can only approximate it by using nouns or infinitive constructions. For instance, *Reading is fun* can be translated

2

Lesen macht Spaß and *It is hard getting up in the mornings* as *Es ist schwer, morgens aufzustehen.* Also English progressive tenses do not have a grammatical counterpart in German. Thus, a translation has to take recourse to a lexical solution to express the special tense meaning of the verb, e.g. *I'm watching the news, can wait for five minutes?* turns into *Ich schaue mir <u>gerade</u> die Nachrichten an, kannst du fünf Minuten warten?* Even if meaning can be conveyed more or less equivalently by different patterns, there is still a loss of grammatical originality and of SL authenticity.

Other untranslatable features of languages are dialects and accents, which exhibit phonetic, lexical and grammatical peculiarities. For instance *Irish, Scottish* or *Welsh* cannot be translated into *Bavarian, Hessian,* or *Saxon* in German. Even if TL dialects are used for stylistic reasons, this method is only a compensation which is, despite all possible underlying parallels, an arbitrary decision connected to a massive loss of uniqueness and authenticity. For instance, the adaptation of the Eliza Doolittle's *Cockney* accent to a *Berlin* or *Viennese* dialect in German versions of the musical *My Fair Lady* (cf. German Wikipedia entry) may be a good equivalence, but it only renders some aspects of Cockney.

Finally, languages are no static but evolving entities (cf. Pym & Turk 2001, 274). Therefore, diachronic semantic and grammatical shifts may occur which pose severe translation problems as illustrated by the translation of historical texts and classical literature. Archaisms and non-standard dialects can be used as equivalents, but again the originality of the SL text is lost in translation, and there is also the danger of a loss of readability and comprehensibility (cf. Venuti 2001, 242). A translation of antiquated SL texts therefore often demands an adaptation in style or a modification in content (cf. Bastin 2001, 7). Sometimes it can even necessitate a new version of the SL text if the translation problems are to severe (cf. Andermann 2001, 72 for literary translation). In this case loss and gain are maximized and the SL text only functions as a template.

As a means of social communication language is furthermore governed by cultural norms, either by specific literary norms or on a larger scale by mentalities or ideologies. Due to cultural, stylistic and ideological differences between source culture (SC) and target culture (TC) some shifts are necessary to adapt the SL text. Contrary to the obligatory linguistic shifts, these shifts are optional and made on a discretionary basis (cf. Bakker, Koster, Van Leuven-Zwart 2001, 288). Therefore, not only loss and gain are involved but also an element of arbitrariness.

Equivalence in literary translation presupposes knowledge about SC and TC, and about their textual and literary conventions (cf. Vermeer 2001, 63; House 2001, 198; Lambert 2001, 132). Due to the fact that translation always aims at the TL audience, an orientation towards TC literary genres and norms is essential. Often "ready-made poetic models" are used which seem to represent the SL text best (cf. Andermann 2001, 72). Even if equivalence is achieved, this technique remains a "domestication" and an "ethnocentric reduction" of the ST to a greater or lesser extent (Schleiermacher cited in Venuti 2001, 242).

Imagery and metaphors are culturally bound, too. Even if there is a TL equivalent, semantic loss or distortions are unavoidable. For instance, the translation of the German saying *zwei Fliegen mit einer Klappe schlagen* into *to kill two birds with one stone* conveys the same basic meaning, namely *'to achieve two goals with one action'*, but its lacks the nuance of *'to get rid of annoying tasks'* that is contained in *Fliegen (flies)*.

Talking names may lose their significance in a translation or their SL usage lacks an effect on the audience. A German translation of the villain *Captain Hook* in M.J. Barrie's novel *Peter Pan* as *Kapitän Haken* would add an unwanted ridiculousness to him. On the other hand the English names of the protagonist *Harry Angel* and his antagonist *Louis Cyphre* (strong phonetic similarity to Lucifer) in Allan Parker's thriller *Angel Heart* lose their allusive character for a German audience.

The translation of humour is another example of the difficulty of adaptations. For instance, the joke *What is black and white and read all over? A newspaper!* would lose its wit in a German translation, because it draws on the ambiguity of the words *read* and *red* which are homophones in English but not in German (*gelesen/rot*). Cultural peculiarities of humour like the cruelty and self-mockery of British humour are hardly translatable for cultures which do not regard these as funny.

Finally, as Wilhelm von Humboldt pointed out, do languages always embody a way of thinking (Humboldt 1796 / 1868: vi cited in Pym & Turk 2001, 273 et seq.). They contain and convey cultural mentalities and ideologies which also comprise certain preferences of language use. Germans for instance have an inclination to nouns and compounds, passive constructions, and complex syntax. Britons rather tend to express meaning with verbs in an active voice which are embedded in a clear word order. This difference accounts for the difficulty of translating the "gravity" of German philosophy into English, especially if the concepts expressed in nouns are novel. Transposition techniques, which render SL words by TL words of different word-classes, can overcome such problems (Bakker, Koster, van Leuven-Zwart 2001, 228) but may lead to shifts in meaning and only barely approximate the

4

precision of the original. Furthermore, an elaboration of unknown SC concepts always occurs on the backdrop of TC notions which can cause distortions or even massive ideological shifts (cf. Andermann 2001, 73; Venuti, 2001, 242).

The complexity of language and the influence of cultural norms complicate the search for optimal equivalences, but the decisive cause for the impossibility of a perfect translation is the human factor in form of the translator and the receptors.

The quality of translation always depends on the knowledge and skills of the translator, which have to comprise linguistic, socio-cultural and stylistic aspects. Due to asymmetric competences in this respect, directionality plays an immense role, since translation into the language of "habitual use" will yield better results in terms of accuracy, naturalness and effectiveness (Beeby Lonsdale 2001, 64). Also the translator's personal preferences, beliefs and values, as well as his class membership influence the translating process (cf. Busch 2001, 128; Wilss 2001, 58 et seq.), e.g. in the choice of syntactic structures and register. In addition, literal translation also relies on the translator's intuition, artistic competence and creativity, which are all subjective traits (cf. House 2001, 197; Bush 2001, 129 et seq.)

Translation as a complex and demanding decision making process also has to face the human tendency to make mistakes. Memory limitations, knowledge and attentional gaps, attitudinal factors and interference effects can cause translation errors (cf. Wilss, 2001, 58). Institutional constraints like deadlines, publisher's directives and house styles can also exert pressure on translators, which affects the translation extent and quality (cf. Beeby Lonsdale 2001, 67; Busch 2001, 128 et seq.; Vermeer 2001, 63).

As the definition of equivalence implied, the quality of translation ultimately depends on an assessment by TL receptors. The respective target group and their expectations define the criteria for acceptability, authenticity and quality in general. A good example is Wolfgang Krege's disputed new translation of J.R.R. Tolkien's *Lord of the Rings* which faced heavy protest from critics and fans alike. Krege intended a modern version which should assimilate Tolkien's opus into German (Krege 2000). The changing of some familiar names and the usage of contemporary terminology and phraseology[1] were regarded by critics as an unacceptable distortion of the original content. Proponents in return claimed that the new version suited the original better than the old antiquated translation by Margaret Carroux (cf. WDR5 Tolkiens Kosmos). This controversy shows that quality is always a relative value

---

[1] For an extensive overview of the differences between the English original and the two German translations see the German Elrond's house website

judgement and largely based on personal taste. Due to this, a perfect translation which lives up to all expectations cannot exist.

Summing up, perfection in terms of translation is not absolute sameness, but a relative equivalence between SL and TL texts. A maximal equivalence cannot be achieved because of linguistic, cultural and stylistic constraints, which bring about some degree of loss or gain in content or form. Furthermore, the individuality and fallibility of translators will always be a source of errors and distortions, but what is more, heterogeneous expectations of the audience rule out a common quality standard and a maximum of acceptability.

Therefore, a perfect translation cannot exist and translating has to be regarded as a quest for near-optimal solutions. But this also has its advantages. Absolute perfection would be static and final. Partial imperfection demands constant debate and negotiation of possible solutions, which fosters the ultimate aim of translation, cross-cultural communication. Moreover, an acceptance of imperfection could shift the focus from what is lost in translation to what can be gained by translating: renunciation of levelling and appreciation of cultural difference.

Reference List

ANDERMANN, GUNILLA. 2001. Drama translation. In: BAKER, MONA and MALMKJAER, KIRSTEN. *Routledge Encyclopedia of Translation Studies*.2001. Routledge: London. pp. 71-74.

ANGEL HEART (1987, Allan Parker, US, 113 mins.)

BAKKER, MATHIJS, KOSTER, CEES and VAN LEUVEN-ZWART, KITTY. 2001. Shifts of translation. In: BAKER, MONA and MALMKJAER, KIRSTEN. *Routledge Encyclopedia of Translation Studies*.2001. Routledge: London. pp.226-231.

BARRIE, J.M.1995. *Peter Pan*. Penguin Books: London

BASTIN, GEORGE L. 2001. Adaptation. In: BAKER, MONA and MALMKJAER, KIRSTEN. *Routledge Encyclopedia of Translation Studies*.2001. Routledge: London. pp.5-8.

BEEBY LONSDALE, ALLISON. 2001. Direction of translation (directionality) In: BAKER, MONA and MALMKJAER, KIRSTEN. *Routledge Encyclopedia of Translation Studies*.2001. Routledge: London. pp.63-67.

BUSCH, PETER. 2001. Literary translation: practices. In: BAKER, MONA and MALMKJAER, KIRSTEN. *Routledge Encyclopedia of Translation Studies*.2001. Routledge: London. pp.127-130.

ELROND'S HOUSE WEBSITE.
Namen & Orte im Herr der Ringe...
Available from: http://www.elronds-haus.de/namen.htm
[Accessed: 19.11.06]

Übersetzungsvergleich
Available from: http://www.elronds-haus.de/translate.htm
[Accessed: 19.11.06]

HARVEY, KEITH. 2001. Compensation. In: BAKER, MONA and MALMKJAER, KIRSTEN. *Routledge Encyclopedia of Translation Studies*.2001. Routledge: London. pp. 37-40.

HOUSE, JULIANE. 2001. Quality of translation. In: BAKER, MONA and MALMKJAER, KIRSTEN. *Routledge Encyclopedia of Translation Studies*.2001. Routledge: London. pp. 197-200.

HUMBOLDT, WILHELM VON. 1796/1868. Brief an A.W. Schlegel vom 23.Juli 1796. In: KLETTE, ANTON. 1868. *Verzeichnis der von A.W. v. Schlegel nachgelassenen Briefsammlung: Nebst Mittheilung ausgewählter Proben des Briefwechsels mit den Gebrüdern von Humboldt, F. Schleiermacher, B. G.B. Niebuhr u. J. Grimm*. Bonn: (no publisher). v-vi. Cited in: PYM, ANTHONY and TURK, HORST. 2001. Translatability. In: BAKER, MONA and MALMKJAER, KIRSTEN. *Routledge Encyclopedia of Translation Studies*.2001. Routledge: London. p. 272 et seq.

KENNY, DOROTHY. 2001. Equivalence. In: BAKER, MONA and MALMKJAER, KIRSTEN. *Routledge Encyclopedia of Translation Studies*.2001. Routledge: London. pp. 77-80.

KREGE, WOLFGANG. 2000. On: Tolkienist.de homepage. *Die Neuübersetzung des Herrn der Ringe.*
Available from: http://www.tolkienist.de/werke_neuuebersetzung.html
[Accessed: 19.11.06]

LAMBERT, JOSÈ. 2001. Literary translation: research issues. In: BAKER, MONA and MALMKJAER, KIRSTEN. *Routledge Encyclopedia of Translation Studies*.2001. Routledge: London. pp. 130-133.

My Fair Lady. *German Wikipedia entry.*
Available from: http://de.wikipedia.org/wiki/My_Fair_Lady
[Accessed: 19.11.06]

PYM, ANTHONY and TURK, HORST. 2001. Translatability. In: BAKER, MONA and MALMKJAER, KIRSTEN. *Routledge Encyclopedia of Translation Studies*.2001. Routledge: London. pp. 271- 276.

ROBINSON, DOGLAS. 2001. Literal translation. In: BAKER, MONA and MALMKJAER, KIRSTEN. *Routledge Encyclopedia of Translation Studies*.2001. Routledge: London. pp.125-127.

VENUTI, LAWRENCE. Strategies of translation. In: BAKER, MONA and MALMKJAER, KIRSTEN. *Routledge Encyclopedia of Translation Studies*.2001. Routledge: London. pp. 240-244.

VERMEER, HANS J. 2001. Didactics of translation. In: BAKER, MONA and MALMKJAER, KIRSTEN. *Routledge Encyclopedia of Translation Studies*.2001. Routledge: London. pp. 60- 63.

WDR5. *Tolkiens Kosmos. Carroux oder Krege? Die Übersetzungen...*
Available from: http://www.wdr5.de/herrderringe/script.phtml?view=menu&page=30.90.00
[Accessed: 19.11.06]

WILSS, WOLFRAM. 2001. Decision making in translation. In: BAKER, MONA and MALMKJAER, KIRSTEN. *Routledge Encyclopedia of Translation Studies*.2001. Routledge: London. pp. 57- 60.

CPSIA information can be obtained
at www.ICGtesting.com
Printed in the USA
LVIC052237310113

318109LV00003B